AF228642

AMELIA EARHART'S LAST FLIGHT

Tim Cooke

Lerner Publications ◆ Minneapolis

Lerner Publications Company
An imprint of Lerner Publishing Group, Inc.
241 First Avenue North
Minneapolis, MN 55401 USA

For reading levels and more information, look up this title at www.lernerbooks.com.

Main body text set in ITC Franklin Gothic.
Typeface provided by International Typeface Corporation.

Library of Congress Cataloging-in-Publication Data

Names: Cooke, Tim, 1961– author.
Title: Amelia Earhart's last flight / Tim Cooke.
Description: Minneapolis : Lerner Publications, [2025] | Series: That's strange! Updog Books | Includes bibliographical references and index. | Audience: Ages 8–11 | Audience: Grades 4–6 |
Summary: "Aviator Amelia Earhart was flying over the Pacific Ocean then was never seen again. Did her plane fall in the water? Did she make it to an island? Readers explore the mystery of Earhart's final flight"— Provided by publisher.
Identifiers: LCCN 2024015183 (print) | LCCN 2024015184 (ebook) | ISBN 9798765648162 (lib. bdg.) | ISBN 9798765662502 (pbk.) | ISBN 9798765658871 (epub)
Subjects: LCSH: Earhart, Amelia, 1897-1937--Juvenile literature. | Aeronautics—Flights—Juvenile literature. | Search and rescue operations—Juvenile literature. | Aircraft accidents—South Pacific Ocean—Juvenile literature. | Women air pilots—United States—Juvenile literature. | Air pilots—United States—Juvenile literature.
Classification: LCC TL540.E3 C67 2025 (print) | LCC TL540.E3 (ebook) | DDC 629.13092—dc23/eng/20240415

LC record available at https://lccn.loc.gov/2024015183
LC ebook record available at https://lccn.loc.gov/2024015184

Manufactured in the United States of America

1 – CG – 12/15/24

Table of Contents

Missing!   4

A Famous Pilot   8

Lost!   18

Where is Earhart?   24

Glossary 30

Check It Out! 31

Index   32

Missing!

Amelia Earhart flew airplanes.

She wanted to fly
around the world.

Earhart preparing to fly

Her airplane disappeared.
She was never seen again.

UP NEXT!

A BIG STAR.

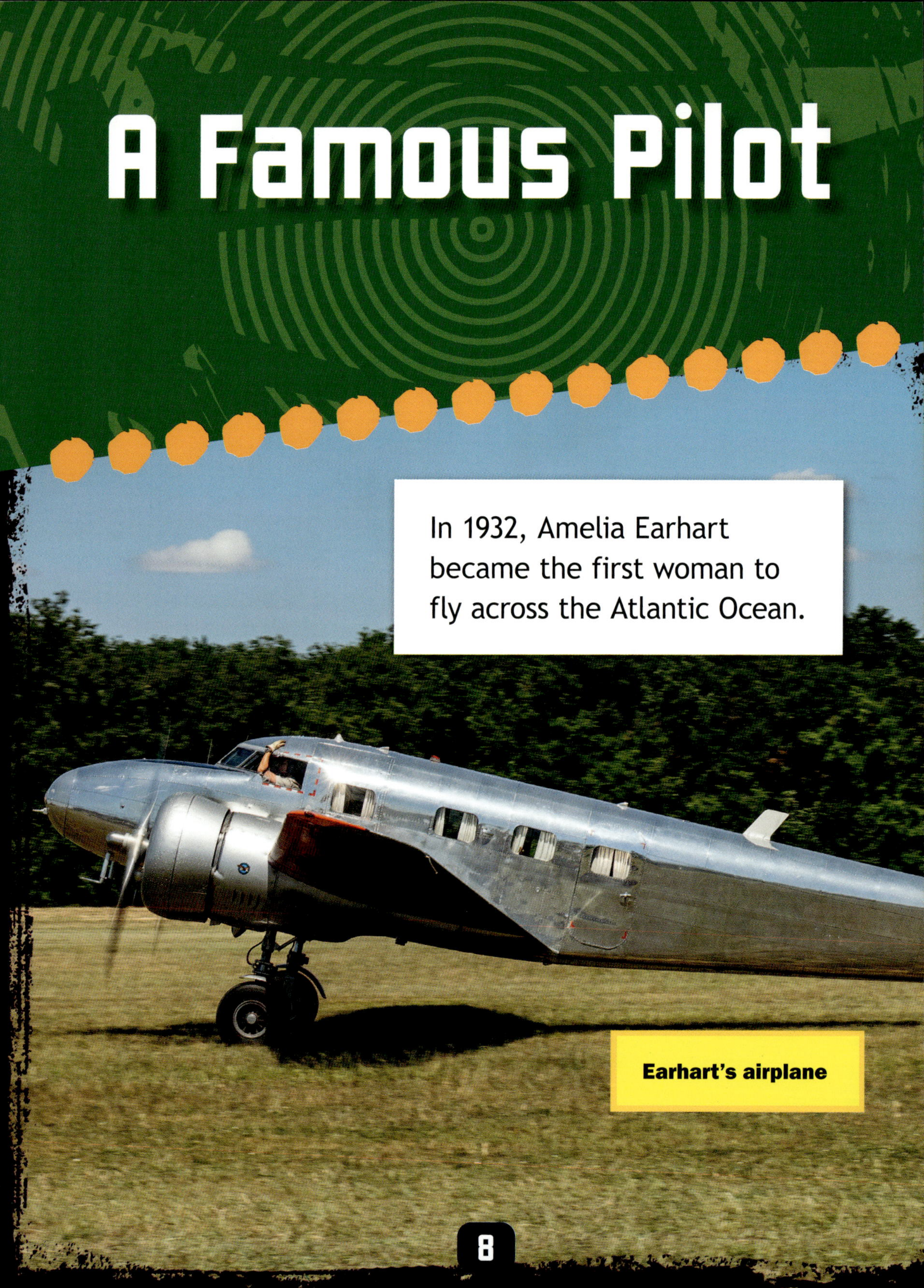

A Famous Pilot

In 1932, Amelia Earhart became the first woman to fly across the Atlantic Ocean.

Earhart's airplane

She flew alone.

Earhart flew solo
from Hawaii to
California in 1935.

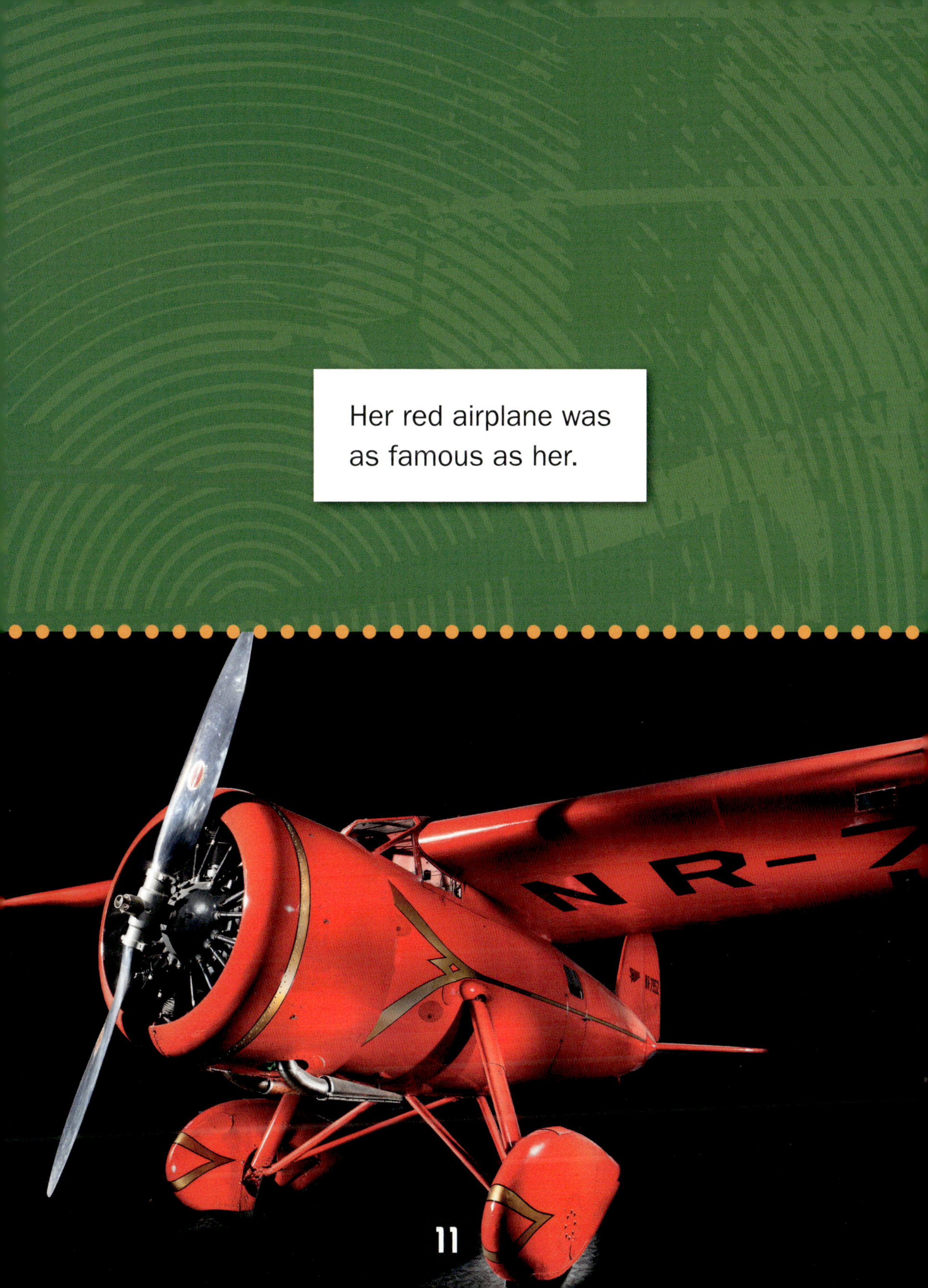

Her red airplane was
as famous as her.

Earhart set bigger goals. She wanted to fly around the world.

In 1937, she was the
first woman to do it.

Earhart planned her trip. She wanted to fly along the equator.

She needed
a strong
airplane with
two engines.

List Break!

- From Miami, Florida, she flew to Africa.

- From Africa she flew to India.

Darwin, Australia

- From India she flew across the Pacific Ocean.

UP NEXT!

FINDING CLUES.

Lost!

Earhart had a
copilot to help her.

The two flew to Papua New
Guinea. The flight was over water.

Earhart then flew toward a tiny island in the middle of the Pacific Ocean.
Howland Island

She would refuel there.

A crowd waited
on the island.

Earhart radioed to say she was low on fuel. Then there was silence.

UP NEXT!

A MYSTERY.

Where is Earhart?

Everyone watched the sky. The plane did not appear.

People hunted for Earhart for
16 days. They found nothing.

Were Earhart and
her copilot alive?

Some people think they landed
on a different island. They could
have survived for a few years.

Other people think
the airplane crashed.

In 2024, a plane was spotted at the bottom of the ocean. Was it Earhart's airplane? We don't know for sure!

Glossary

copilot: someone who helps a pilot fly an airplane

engine: a machine that makes something move

equator: the way around Earth at its widest point

refuel: to fill back up with gasoline

solo: one person on their own

Check It Out!

Academic Kids: Amelia Earhart
https://academickids.com/encyclopedia/index.php/Amelia_
Earhart

Conley, Kate A. *Amelia Earhart*. Minneapolis: Abdo, 2022.

Gagliardi, Sue. *Amelia Earhart*. Mendota Heights, MN: Apex
Editions, 2023.

Kiddle: Amelia Earhart Facts for Kids
https://kids.kiddle.co/Amelia_Earhart

Krensky, Stephen. *Amelia Earhart*. New York: Crabtree,
2023.

Social Studies for Kids: Amelia Earhart
https://socialstudiesforkids.com/articles/ushistory
/ameliaearhart1.htm

Index

airplane, 4, 7–8, 11, 15, 28–29
Atlantic Ocean, 8

fuel, 21, 23

island, 20, 22, 27

Pacific Ocean, 6, 17, 20

Photo Acknowledgments

Image credits: ersin ergin/Shutterstock, pp. 3 (top), 23 (bottom); www.thestar.com/ Wikimedia Commons, pp. 3 (bottom), 9; www.airandspace.si.edu/, p. 46; Kit8.net, p. 5; Luciaroblego Wikimedia Commons, p. 6; MMPOP/Shutterstock, p. 7; Simon Vandamme/Shutterstock, p. 8; Drone Northwest/Shutterstock, p. 10; Smithsonian Institute/Wikimedia Commons, p. 11; www.digital.library.ucla.edu/ Wikimedia Commons, p. 12; Everett Collection/Shutterstock, pp. 13, 15, 18, 22, 23; Dimitrios Karamitros/Shutterstock, p. 14; Michal Izydorczyk/Shutterstock, p. 16 (top); Art-is-Power/Shutterstock, p. 16 (bottom); Daniel Mitchel/Shutterstock, p. 17; Danita Delimont/Shutterstock, p. 19; USFWS/Wikimedia Commons, p. 20; Supertrooper/ Shutterstock, p. 21; Sergey Tinyakov/Shutterstock, p. 24; Sarinee58/Shutterstock, p. 25; Wikimedia Commons, p. 26; kwest/Shutterstock, p. 27; Christopher Buff/ Shutterstock, p. 28; Melnikov Dmitriy/Shutterstock, p. 29. Design elements: sokolovski/Shutterstock, pp. 1–32.
Cover: sokolovski/Shutterstock; Everett Collection/Shutterstock; Wadim Wall/ Shutterstock.